Stink fight

Fossa chase

Hawk
attack

Sunbath

Storm

Plays with cousin

Tamarind pod

Sleep trees

# A Little Lemur Named Mew

## Joyce A. Powzyk

THE MILLBROOK PRESS

Brookfield, Connecticut

 *This book is dedicated to my own little primate family,
Stephen, Audra, and Clark*

Published by The Millbrook Press, Inc.
2 Old New Milford Road
Brookfield, Connecticut 06804
www.millbrookpress.com

Library of Congress Cataloging-in-Publication Data
Powzyk, Joyce Ann.
A little lemur named Mew / Joyce A. Powzyk.
p. cm.
Summary: Follows the life of a young ring-tailed lemur and his troop in the
forests of Madagascar.
ISBN 0-7613-2665-0 (lib. bdg.)
1. Ring-tailed lemur—Juvenile literature. [1. Ring-tailed lemur.  2. Lemurs.
3. Animals—Infancy.]  I. Title.
QL737.P95 P695 2003   599.8'3—dc21   2002012031

My name is Mew. I am a young ring-tailed lemur. I came into the world late one night, high up in a tree where my mother licked me and kept me warm. I was very tiny then—no bigger than a newborn kitten.

My mom and I live with a lemur troop, our family. There are ten of us in all, including some other youngsters. I know them all. Each ring-tail has a different look, a different smell. My mom is head of the group. She is Topmom. All the lemurs run from her, including the big males.

Come with me as I learn about my family and this place where I was born.

My home is a large dry forest on a remote island called Madagascar off the coast of Africa. This forest has tall trees and some open areas. We live in both. Our troop likes to play on the thick tangled vines that hang from the trees.

Besides seeing the many shades of green in my forest, I can also smell it. There is the sweet smell of new leaves and flowers and the earthy smell of soil. A large winding river curves through the landscape, and our forest hugs this river, drawing up its moisture through the trees' deep roots.

This forest is also home to many other kinds of animals. There are colorful birds, large fruit bats, huge snakes, and catlike fossas. Different types of lemurs also live here, such as the brown lemurs who have dark faces and long brown tails. Some of these animals scare me, but others are fun to watch and I can even play with a few.

Today I am ten weeks old. I've grown a lot since being born—I'm almost twice as big. I awake and look into the face of my mother. Her large brown eyes blink slowly back at me. The morning air is cold. I touch noses with my mom. Then I'll snuggle into the warmth of her fur. Mom's scent is strong.

Our troop has spent the night in a large tamarind tree. This is one of our favorite sleep trees because it is tall with big wide branches for sitting. There are dark shadows on the forest floor, and I peer down at them, nervous and excited. I wonder what is hiding in the leaves and what the day will bring.

Nearby, the other lemurs stretch and yawn. Two males start to amble along the branch and back down the tree, tail end first. Mother gives a few short "mew, mew, me-ow" calls and starts to climb down herself. I clutch her chest tightly, not wanting to fall.

When our troop reaches the ground, all the older lemurs sit down, facing the sun, with their bellies exposed and arms out. I try to copy my mother. Ahhh! A wave of warmth moves over my body as the sun hits my skin. Although days may be hot in this place, the nights can be cold, and this is how we warm ourselves in the morning.

We are hungry now. It's time to search for food! Topmom finds a pod that has fallen from a tamarind tree, cracks it open, and chews the sticky substance inside. I push my muzzle into her face and lick the food. So tangy! I shake my head as my tongue takes in the bitter taste. We eat a lot of this sour food, but I am also beginning to eat the young leaves of the tamarind tree as well. My mom teaches me what is good to eat.

Topmom lets me snatch her food while she searches for another pod. As I sit chewing, I hear many birds fluttering in the branches. All are chattering and singing as they, too, search for something to eat. Ouch! I reach around and catch a biting insect in my fur. I pop it into my mouth—crunchy!

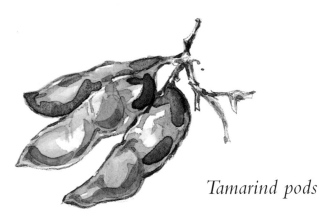

*Tamarind pods*

Topmom has had enough tamarind. She moves out of the tree and the other lemurs join us. We're off to another food tree.

Every day I feel bigger and stronger. As mom is walking, I leap onto her leg and pull myself up, one fistful of fur after another. Finally I'm up on her back. Whew! I did it!

From Topmom's back I can see all the lemurs walking, their tails held high in the air. With these striped tails in view, I feel safe, surrounded by my troop. Every lemur in my group has a long tail except for Stumpy. He lost part of his tail in a fight with a male from a neighboring group. I like my long fluffy tail. It helps me balance, but it also keeps me warm. I wrap it around my body when I sleep.

As we move through the forest, we pass some of my cousins. I jump off Topmom's back and run to Softtail with my mouth open in a play face. I grab her fur and give it a quick pull. Then I start back toward Topmom, my protector. Can't catch me. But before I get to safety, Softtail jumps on top of me and we roll across the ground. All this play is fun, and I learn to jump and pounce better every day.

Oh no, here comes Sharptooth. He wants to play, too, and bites my ear. I push him away with a scolding trill from my throat, but he bites me again, only harder. Sharptooth plays too rough for me and Softtail. I hide behind Topmom. Sharptooth starts to come toward me again, but Topmom gives him a serious look and away he runs.

The morning goes by quickly. Soon it is midday. The sun is hot and the drone of the insects is loud in my ears. Mom begins to groom me. This feels good. My eyes close. Groom me, groom me some more. Each day Topmom grooms my fur, cleaning it with her bottom teeth and taking out all those bad things like sticky seeds.

After my grooming, Topmom and I move up on a shady branch where the other lemurs are huddled closely in a row. It's hard to tell where one lemur ends and another begins.

A yawn escapes from my mouth as my eyes droop from sleepiness. I push my snout under Topmom's arm and drink some milk. Then I drift off to sleep, making little purring noises in my throat. But when a bird screeches, my head pops up. We ring-tails are always watchful.

After a long nap, everyone is hungry again. The troop moves out, leaping from tree to tree. The older lemurs know where the food is, so they lead the group.

Before long, we come upon a ficus tree heavy with sweet fruit. Topmom gets the best feeding spot. A male comes too close and she cuffs him on the head. He squeals and backs away. Even though I'm little, I get to feed on the sweetest fruit because I'm next to Topmom, who is dominant over the other lemurs in our troop.

Suddenly, the forest is alive with shrieking lemur calls. We all look up to see a large hawk gliding just above the treetops. The adults continue their alarm calls as their tails swing back and forth nervously.

I am intrigued by this animal that can fly. I climb up on a high branch to get a better look. Then I hear a swooshing noise behind me as another hawk flies by. I get scared and scramble back to Topmom who is sitting in a sheltered spot beneath the branch. That was close!

I stay beside Topmom for a while, but my nervousness doesn't last long. Soon I discover a thin branch that easily bends back and forth, and I swing by my feet, enjoying this tipsy feeling.

In the late afternoon, the sun begins to drop behind the tall trees. This is our signal that night is about to fall. Topmom starts to leave for our sleep site without me and I squeal in protest, "eekkk!" She stops and looks over her shoulder as I race to jump on her back. That's better.

I'm enjoying the ride as we leap through the forest when we hear the other lemurs bark alarm calls. Below us on the ground is a big brown creature, a fossa, and its eyes are fixed on Topmom and me.

Topmom quickens her pace. I can feel her muscles moving beneath her fur. I clutch her tightly. We've never moved so fast. We travel for a long time and finally arrive at the river's edge where the trees are huge.

We rest in a large mahogany tree, breathing heavily. I look to the faces of the others in my group. Is it safe? The other ring-tails seem calm and start to groom one another, but I still feel nervous and keep looking around. My eyes will be the last to close this night.

Several days have passed. We're back to our normal routine—we sleep, we eat, we play, and we explore. I begin to forget about the scary fossa that chased us.

One afternoon while our troop is nibbling on some hackberry plants, I notice two males staring at each other. I sit up on my haunches to get a better view.

Stinker's ears flatten as a deep purr rises up from his throat. He pulls his tail between his wrists and gets it good and stinky with scent from glands on his wrists. Then he takes a step forward and arches his tail, which begins to quiver and wave in the air.

Snuff arches his tail and waves it back at Stinker. After a few moments, Snuff gives a short "yip" and runs away. Stinker is a very stinky lemur and he has won. The air is heavy with the males' scent.

This is a stink fight! It is like a fight, but neither of the lemurs touches one another. When I get big, I'll have my own stink fights and beat all the other males.

Later a group of brown lemurs comes out of the forest into our clearing. The adults make deep husky grunts as they look around cautiously.

A young brown lemur about my size runs out from the group and freezes as we come face-to-face. Our eyes are fixed on each other. Is he going to hurt me? Should I run away? I look to Topmom who is watching me but continues to nibble a leaf. She doesn't look alarmed so I decide that this lemur must be okay.

I puff up my chest and try to look big. Then I charge the young lemur. It leaps into the air. Back and forth we go, having our pretend fight. Eventually the brown lemurs head back into the forest. I stare at them and want to give chase, but I have a stronger pull to stay with my own kind.

🌿 In a few months, the weather begins to change. It is the beginning of the rainy season. Today the air is moist and the sky is dark gray. Everywhere there is movement as the trees sway in the wind. Soon rain begins to pour down on me as I sit on my sleep branch. Everything is becoming blurry and dark.

I look around for Topmom and can't find her. I start to run but slip on the wet bark and land in the bushes below.

I see a striped tail before me. It's Sharptooth! The forest has become a frightening place. Sharptooth and I start running, faster and faster. From behind we hear a giant tree falling. The wood cracks and splinters, and then *THUMP*, the ground shakes. WHERE is Topmom? It seems to take forever before we find her.

Dawn breaks over the forest. The cyclone has passed. During the night, Sharptooth and I huddled with Topmom. We awake to a green-blue sky. The air is calm. I notice that several big trees have fallen, and there is light where there was once only darkness.

I stoop to lick some water that is pooling on a large leaf. A boa slithers by and I jump back. The giant snake probably was sleeping in the tree that came down. The forest is full of surprises.

Our troop is back together, and all the cousins begin to chase one another. I climb onto a huge tree trunk. We will explore these fallen trees for days, and I will be king of the tree. Just try to knock me off my perch!

# Lemur Facts

❀ There are more than thirty kinds of lemurs, some as small as a mouse while the largest, weighing in at 14 pounds (6.4 kilograms), is about the size of a large domestic cat. Adult ring-tails weigh from 6 to 8 pounds (2.7 to 3.7 kilograms). All lemurs are quick moving and have large round eyes and soft coats of fur.

❀ Lemurs are primates, meaning they are related to monkeys, but they do not swing in trees the way monkeys do. Rather they leap from tree to tree. They have relatively small brains, yet are successful in living in every type of island forest—dry lowland, spiny, and lush.

❀ Lemurs eat a variety of foods, including leaves, flowers, fruit, insects, and tree sap. They all have a strong sense of smell and specialized glands on their body that produce scent, but only the ring-tails have stink fights where males face off and waft scent at each other.

❀ Ring-tailed lemurs live in a society in which adult females are dominant over adult males. This is unusual in the world of primates. They have a special adaptation for grooming known as a toothcomb. Their lower teeth are close set all in a row, and they run this through their fur to keep it clean and tidy.

❀ Lemurs have numerous predators, including the Malagasy Harrier Hawk and the fossa. Ring-tails have different alarm calls for different predators. They give a shrieking call for predators from above and a barking call for predators on the ground. Only 40 percent of young ring-tails survive to adulthood.

❀ At one time, ancestors to the lemurs inhabited much of the Earth, but, today, lemurs are rare and endangered. They are found only on the island of Madagascar, off the southeast coast of Africa. There they exist in an ever-disappearing habitat. The forests on Madagascar are under pressure to be cut for timber and for farming and grazing, yet their preservation is vital if wild lemurs are to survive for the long term.

AFRICA

MADAGASCAR

❀ Ring-tails are among the world's best known lemurs, in part because they adapt well to captivity and can be seen at almost 150 zoos around the world.